# PORTRAITS OF 'KINGS'

Portraits of every Western Region 'King' Class locomotive
in single and double chimney form, with footplate comments.

Bryan Holden

&

Kenneth H. Leech

BSc, CEng, FICE, FIMech E

With additional research & drawings by Richard S. Potts

FRASER STEWART

This 1990 edition published for
Fraser Stewart Book Wholesale Ltd,
Abbey Chambers, 4 Highbridge Street,
Waltham Abbey, Essex EN9 1DQ

ISBN 0 903485 93 1

Printed in England by Clays Ltd, St Ives plc

# PORTRAITS OF 'KINGS'

*From an original oil painting by Richard S. Potts.*

# Contents

# Acknowledgement

Sincere thanks are expressed to Richard (Dick) Potts for his help in the preparation of this book, particularly his researches into *King* modifications and for supplying diagrammatic drawings.

An engine driver formerly on BR Western Region, working out of the old GWR steam shed at Tyseley, Birmingham, Dick Potts's experience and first-hand knowledge has been of inestimable value.

Also to A. L. Hammonds ARCA, ATD, RBSA for additional illustrations, and Harold Parsons for checking the manuscript.

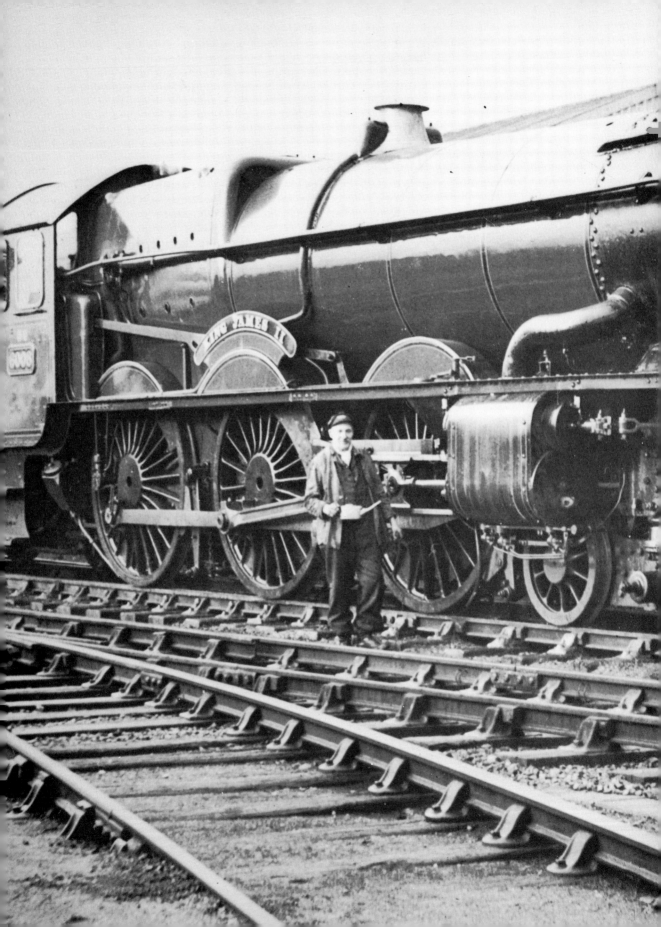

# Introduction

Much has been written on the design and building of the Great Western's *King* class locomotives. There is ample printed evidence of their performance during almost forty years of express passenger train working. Certainly, there is no shortage of pictorial documentation, for these thirty engines have surely been photographed more than any pop singer, filmstar or sporting hero.

*Portraits of Kings* is not a technical treatise, neither is it a record of locomotive practice and performance or a random collection of *King* photographs. Its *raison d'etre* is a singular man of action, Kenneth Leech, to whom steam traction has always been of compelling interest.

During World War II his work took him to Chippenham, Wiltshire, near the Great Western's London to Bristol railway line. This rekindled an interest in steam locomotives and over the next two decades, in his spare time, he was to amass a collection of more than 20,000 photographs of GWR engines.

Retirement afforded him more opportunity to indulge this interest. He made friends of locomotive drivers and firemen, and travelled over 45,000 miles with them on the footplates of express passenger engines. He rode on every one of the thirty *Kings* usually firing or driving, and he came to know the idiosyncrasies of each engine better than most of us understand those of our own motor car.

In recounting some of Kenneth Leech's footplate experiences, and in bringing together for the first time the cream of his *King* photographic collection, this book aims to convey something of the personality of those mighty engines and give an insight into the characters of men who worked them, as a reminder of the great days when steam was king.

Bryan Holden
Solihull
June 1979

# Profile of Kenneth H. Leech

It was 7029 *Clun Castle* that introduced me to Kenneth Leech. At the time I was seeking photographs of this famous engine taken during the fifteen years of its working life before it was withdrawn from service in December 1965, when it was purchased privately and came to the Birmingham Railway Museum.

Such a quest was bound to lead me eventually to Kenneth Leech, well known for his comprehensive photographic coverage of the express locomotive stud of the former Great Western Railway throughout the West Country and at Swindon Works. Never was he able to understand my enthusiasm for those old photographs: 'At Tyseley, you have the real *Clun Castle*', he would say. But it was always exciting to receive his prints and admire their expert picture composition. Of course, they are irreplaceable, for preservation has changed the very nature of the remaining steam engines; and steam sheds, locomotive sidings and much of the lineside scene has vanished.

It was a footnote to one of his letters that brought about our first meeting: 'If I were your age and you were mine (he was born in 1892), I would expect to visit you,' he wrote. Some weeks later, when I began gathering together material for a series of BBC railway programmes, I went to Chippenham to interview him.

In his 'railway room', as Kenneth called his study, I admired his scale models of Great Northern locomotives which were, he confessed, his first love. Our conversation touched on his rock climbing expeditions to North Wales, the Lake District and the Scottish Highlands; on his musical accomplishments (several of his orchestral works have been broadcast on radio), and on the fact that he had composed some one hundred and thirty songs. Compared to these achievements his involvement in railway matters might have seemed a mild flirtation. Not so, for his interest in railways and steam engines had begun at the age of two, when he was given a model locomotive by his father.

Kenneth Leech was ten years old when he started going by train to school, and he has since made models of the various engines that took him there and brought him back. It was that daily train journey which made him aware of all the different engines, and set him wondering if it might be possible for him to become a locomotive engineer.

On leaving school he spent two years at an engineering day college, after which he became a pupil of Robert Whitelegg, the Locomotive Superintendent of the London, Tilbury & Southend Railway. It was a small company, later taken over by the Midland and subsequently absorbed into the LMS. In those days it had eighty two locomotives. They were kept in the most perfect condition possible, for everything was under the immediate and direct eye of the autocratic Robert Whitelegg.

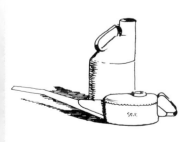

*On the other side of the lens! Kenneth H Leech. January 1958*

Just before young Kenneth finished his pupilage the Midland Railway took over and he was transferred to the running sheds, working as a fitter with special reference to pistons, slide valves and safety valves. 'I well remember those safety valves; flat-seated, very awkward to grind-in properly and to make steam-tight. Although I have been engaged in engineering design all my life, I never again used a flat seat for that type of valve.'

Graduating from running shed to footplate he became a locomotive fireman working 60 hours a week for 24s. It was for him a glorious time: 'I remember my first aiming at the firehole resulted in hitting the side of it. The driver immediately went to his toolbox, took out a hammer and chisel and remarked: "Make it what size you think you'll want it, mate!" So even in those days there was joy on the footplate.'

Kenneth demonstrated for me the skill he had acquired. Digging into an imaginary tender, he mimed his smooth practised action as, legs astride, he rode the bouncing footplate, lifting 20 lb of coal on a 9in shovel. To fire a Great Western express engine was no task for a mere enthusiast; it demanded skill and knowledge, as well as physical endurance. The first two qualities came from a lifetime's experience with the steam locomotive, but the physical aspect was perhaps unusual when possessed to such a degree by a man in his retirement years. A *King* driven hard could beat him, he said, but he could always manage a *Castle!*

Kenneth joined the army in 1916 and served in the Railway Operating Division, first as a millwright and later as a locomotive officer. Returning to civilian life, he entered the drawing office of the Westinghouse Brake & Signal Company as a designer. He had wanted an outdoor job, but never succeeded, and he ultimately became Chief Mechanical Engineer.

By 1921 he had become Chief Draughtsman, and at that point his youthful enthusiasm was diverted temporarily from railways to motor cycles. He became engrossed in building and modifying internal combustion engines, and totally committed himself to the quest for greater speed and improved performance on two wheels.

During World War II, when Kenneth Leech was sent to Chippenham to take charge of Admiralty contracts, his office window overlooked the main line of the Great Western Railway. It was not long before the sight and sound of *Star*s and *Saint*s, *Castle*s and *King*s brought back all his old enthusiasm for steam engines. He found there was a regular running-in turn from Swindon that came though Chippenham at 5.40 every evening, often with a new *Castle* or *King* straight out of the works. This was the start of a great adventure.

'I couldn't help being fascinated by the 30in stroke of the *Saint*s, and it was *Hillingdon Court* that first took my fancy. So I began taking photographs of Great Western engines, and then the drivers asked me for copies and I made them 10in x 8in prints. They invited me to make footplate trips. I refused for a time, but after my first ride on *Lady of Quality* I got rather adventurous. I then did about 2,700 trips on Great Western engines, equal to some 45,000 miles.'

His meticulously detailed log book lists runs on 149 *Castle*s, all thirty *King*s, and on many other classes of Great Western engine. But his involvement with steam locomotives extended far beyond the footplate: over the years his photographic collection had grown to massive proportions. Although he gave away many of his prints to his footplate friends, it became increasingly difficult storing and cataloguing over 20,000 negatives. He was working five nights a week in his darkroom, and in just over five years had purchased more than 16,000 sheets of printing paper!

Most of Kenneth Leech's photographs show the engine driver or fireman, sometimes both, in a conspicuous position. There are thousands of these footplate studies, each man differently and individually attired, his mode of dress, stance and facial expression revealing some facet of his character and personality. These photographs prove that the enginemen were themselves of as much interest to Kenneth as the locomotives, and it is this combination of man and machine that makes his contribution to railway photography such an important social document.

Although he travelled widely on locomotives throughout the West Country, visited Swindon frequently, and was familiar with many main line stations, his favourite spot was Chippenham on the evening running-in turn. Then there would usually be a brand new engine, straight from the works, its copper and brasswork gleaming; often its varnish had not even been rubbed down. The driver would run the engine clear of the platform while Kenneth took photographs.

There were occasions when he drove or fired crack expresses and there were many runs on mixed traffic engines, as well as on Saturday 'shoppers' like the local stopping trains between Chippenham and Bath. But it was the power and magnificence of the *King*s that really caught his imagination.

'*Castle*s, although they have a most glorious record, were by no means as speedy as *King*s. At anything over eighty three miles an hour you had to work them a little bit harder than they seemed to like. A *King* would run up to ninety on the level without any signs of distress, or quivering through its fabric.'

The grand adventure of steam ended in 1962 when Kenneth Leech photographed the last *King* through Chippenham, for soon they were withdrawn. No more would they blast out of Box Tunnel, whistle screaming, smoke and steam clouds billowing above the tree-tops, sunlight glinting on their copper crowns.

There is one picture in Kenneth Leech's golden treasury that occasions from him a heavy sigh. Taken at Swindon, it shows blackened and rusting *King*s awaiting removal to the breakers' yards. There is a sprinkling of dry snow between the tracks, on the buffer beams, and in the crevices along the boilers of the slumbering giants. Their fires are long since dead, their ashes lie scattered in frozen mounds. A truly desolate scene.

'Put it back in the box', said Kenneth, taking this particular photograph from me. 'The whole adventure was such a happy and exciting one, we mustn't get morbid or depressed. Let's talk about my run on the down *Bristolian* with 6015. . . .'

Then came the idea: why not a book on Kenneth Leech's beloved *King*s? Why not, indeed. . . .

# King or Supercastle?
## —the building of the Kings

The first *King* class locomotive made its debut in 1927. Designed by C.B. Collett, Chief Mechanical Engineer of the Great Western Railway, successor to the almost legendary George Jackson Churchward, it was soon derided by detractors as being little more than a *Super-Castle*. Even dyed-in-the-wool GWR devotees raised their eyebrows a little at the specifications of the new class, for in many ways the *King*s were a contradiction of the Great Western's standardisation policy.

Certainly, Churchward's basic design principles had been followed, and the new class had direct lineage through the *Star*s and *Castle*s, but there were numerous changes from standard dimensions. The firebox was lengthened and the grate area increased. Likewise, the boiler barrel was lengthened, increased in diameter, and strengthened to withstand a working pressure of 250 lb/in². To accommodate these new dimensions the wheelbase was extended and, in consequence, longer connecting rods were fitted.

Although the only major departure from Churchward's basic designs was in the bogie, where independent springing was fitted to the four axle boxes, Collett departed from almost every Swindon Works standard in major components: even the bogie wheel diameter was changed by two inches, only valve gear parts remaining essentially the same.

There seems little doubt that Collett conceived the *King*s under pressure from Great Western Board members, in particular from Felix Pole, general manager. In his autobiography *(Felix Pole—His Book)*, Sir Felix refers to the building of the *King*s:

'At the time one of the directors was Sir Aubrey Brocklebank, whose knowledge of locomotive practice was considerable and whose interest in all railway matters profound. Sir Aubrey and I had many talks and were on most intimate terms. In our various conversations he had indicated that locomotives of the *Castle* class were not entirely satisfactory. I forget his point of criticism. . . .'

It is significant that Sir Felix makes no reference to Collett, who as the designer of the *Castle* class would surely have been the one person to know whether they were 'not entirely satisfactory'. And can Sir Aubrey's point of criticism on so an important a matter have been forgotten by Pole?

It seems likely that Sir Aubrey referred to the fact that the *Castle*s were originally intended to take the 4700 class boiler, as had been laid down diagrammatically by Churchward in his proposal for an enlarged *Star,* but that this boiler would have made the engines heavier than the civil engineer could accept, and that a smaller and lighter boiler had to be put on the *Castle*s — a compromise job.

The conclusion that may be drawn from this situation is that Felix Pole saw the *King*s primarily as a major GWR publicity boost to put the Southern Railway's *Lord Nelson* class well and truly in the shade for daring to exceed the tractive effort of the Great Western's *Castle,* and in laying claim to the coveted title:Britain's most powerful express passenger locomotive.

*Super-Castle*s or otherwise, the *King*s soon claimed the lion's share of the news headlines, and the first of the new class, 6000 *King George V,* was shipped to America at the invitation of the Baltimore and Ohio Railroad Company at whose centenary celebrations it was to win international acclaim, and be seen by no less than 1¼ million visitors to the show.

The *New York Herald Tribune* was lyrical about the English *King* even before it had arrived in America: 'Breathes there a man with soul so dead that he doesn't thrill a little at such news? Especially when he learns that this engine, now under construction, will be capable of a speed of eighty miles an hour, the most powerful locomotive ever built for an English railway.' But in spite of plaudits earned by *King George V* in America and the wide acclaim accorded the *King*s at special Swindon Works Open Days, the 'knockers' were never truly silenced. If *King*s are such a success, why have no more than thirty been built? they asked. And the fact that *Castle*s continued to roll out of Swindon 'A' shop right up to 1950 posed the question: Was it because *King*s were really no better than the uniquitous *Castle*?

The Great Western did not deign to reply to such criticism. It let the *King*s and their 40,300 tractive effort speak for themselves, particularly in their performance over the stiff gradients of the West Country main line with heavily-ladened holiday trains. In fact in the early 'thirties, *King*s were taking trains of 360 tons as against the 315 tons limit for *Castle*s over this section; and the twenty-seven year old timing of 247 minutes of the *Cornish Riviera Limited* from Paddington to Plymouth was reduced to the even four hours.

Surprisingly, many of the *King*s best performances were recorded in their last years of service when fitted with four-row superheaters and double blast pipe and chimney. With these final BR modifications, made primarily to maintain performance on poorer coal, the locomotives became virtually *Super King*s.

But always a question mark will hang over the reason for their conception. Would C.B. Collett have built them but for pressure from Felix Pole and his colleagues? Was the *King* really an ace played by a publicity-minded and egocentric Great Western directorate? We shall never know the answer now that the days of *King*s are past. But no doubt such argument and conjecture will continue to stimulate the curious.

# Engine Modifications

The thirty locomotives which comprised the *King* class of the Great Western Railway were built at Swindon Works in two batches between 1927 and 1930; and very little change took place in their appearance until after nationalisation in 1948. Many of the later modifications were small; but others, such as improved draughting and additional superheating were considerable, and transformed the *King*s both in outward appearance and performance.

## GWR modifications

One major point of the initial design proved awkward, namely bogie frame clearance on curves if the inside cylinders were to remain horizontal. This was solved by the use of outside bearings and frames for the leading bogie wheels only, but this unusual feature involved the use of a short separate plate spring for each wheel and led to trouble at first. Track irregularities and engine pitching tended to put an excessive load on these springs, resulting in breakages and hot axleboxes and, indeed, in a derailment luckily not too serious in its consequences, until additional coil springs were provided at the ends of the original plate springs. The original Cartazzi trailing axleboxes were abandoned in favour of axleboxes without sideplay. It made all the difference to the riding of the *King*s at speed.

Nevertheless the final solution of the *King*s as a beautifully smooth riding class of locomotive was found only after a year or two, when the trailing coupled wheel springs were redesigned to give the utmost flexibility by the use of a very large number of thin plates. The *King*s then became among the best riding locomotives in Britain.

Until 1948 there were no further changes in any details of the design and the engines steamed well, were economical on fuel and ran appreciably more freely than the *Castle*s. Perhaps, in some respects, pre-war Swindon Works could be accused of resting on its laurels. But with its premier express passenger locomotives so enthusiastically acclaimed there seemed no reason to seek improvement just for the sake of it.

In contrast to the LNER and the LMS, both of which went the whole hog, the GWR only dabbled in streamlining. In 1935, 6014 *King Henry VII* appeared with a bullet-nose. Fortunately, this half-hearted attempt at streamlining was not extended to other *King*s and was, in fact, removed a bit at a time, until by 1947 all that remained was the wedge-shaped cab front, ventilators in the roof (Fig 1), together with the modified oil-cup bracket on the inside valve casing (Fig 2). This bracket was for attaching the train identity number frame, for when the smokebox had its bulbous nose the frame could not be attached to the smokebox door.

There were several other minor variations: 6001 *King Edward VII* had a smaller right-hand cab side window than the other *King*s (Fig 3), with the idea of enabling the window to be readily cleaned inside in spite of the fitting of the then new Automatic Train Control apparatus inside the cab; lifting holes were drilled in the front framing (Fig 4), and, in an attempt to keep the leading axle boxes cool, a slotted front stretcher was fitted to one bogie unit which was used under several different members of the class (Fig 5).

## BR modifications

The transformation of the *King*s began in 1947 under the direction of F.W.Hawksworth, the last Chief Mechanical Engineer of the Great Western Railway, who instituted tests in the Swindon Experimental Department, during which 6022 *King Edward III* was fitted with a four-row superheated boiler which showed a small but definite improvement over the original design, particularly in regard to water consumption.

When Hawksworth retired in 1949, this work was carried on by his long-serving Swindon colleague, K.J.Cook, until he was transferred to Doncaster in 1951. Surprisingly, Cook's place at Swindon was taken by a North Eastern Railway man, R.A.Smeddle, under whom the most dramatic changes in *King* performance and appearance took place.

But to go back to 1947, 6022 was also the first *King* to be fitted with a mechanical lubricator

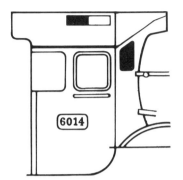

Fig. 1.

Wedge-shape cab on 6014. The only part that remained from its 'streamlined' condition.

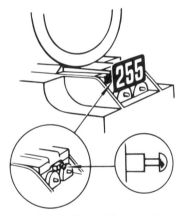

Fig. 2.

On 6014 only. Fitted with 'bullet-nose' streamlining in 1935, the train identity numbers, when introduced, could not be attached to the smokebox door. A bracket was fitted to the inside steam chest cover, where an oil box for spindle lubrication was normally fitted, and the frame for these numbers was clamped onto it.

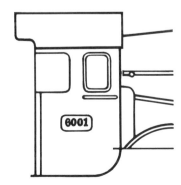

Fig. 3.

Small side window on 6001 only.

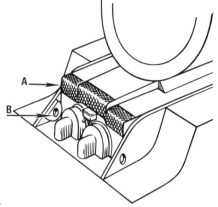

Fig. 4.

Diamond steel plate (A) welded on to top corner to provide foothold for maintenance staff.

Holes (B) cut in frames for lifting by crane. A strengthening piece was fitted later.

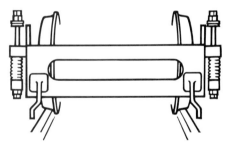

Fig. 5.

Slotted front crossbeam of one bogie frame. Used beneath several members on the class at different times, it gave extra cooling to the axleboxes.

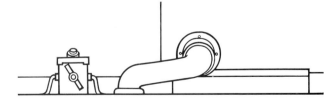

Fig. 6.

First position of mechanical lubricator. Eventually moved to forward position, as it previously restricted access to inside motion.
Original pattern outside steam pipe.

(Fig 6) and the lubricating pipes from the boiler into the smokebox were then covered by a large box (Fig 7).

Mechanical lubricators were introduced so as to take the oiling of cylinders and valves out of the hands of the driver, for with high superheat engines too much oil would carbonise and choke-up steam ports and blast pipe, while too little oil would mean excess wear or actual failure of a part. A mechanical lubricator was set by the works to feed the right amount of oil to each part.

Although it cannot really be classed as a modification, a colour change took place in 1948 when 6009 *King Charles II* and 6025 *King Henry III* appeared in dark blue (virtually GER blue), with red, cream and grey lining out, and with 'British Railways' in plain yellow lettering on the tender. Only six other *King*s received this experimental livery before a lighter shade of Caledonian blue appeared with black and white lining out, received by all the class before a welcome return to Brunswick Green in 1952.

Also in 1948 a square-edged step welded to the top corner of the inside valve cover (Fig 4) was introduced to prevent footplate and shed staff slipping when working in and around the smokebox.

During the period 1949-51, all the *King*s had their boilers rebuilt with four-row superheaters and mechanical lubricators were fitted (Fig 8).

Deterioration in the quality of coal available led to the next development of the class, the redesign of the blastpipe and chimney arrangements. In 1952, 6001 *King Edward VII* and 6017 *King Edward IV* were the first to have their original chimney and jumper-top blastpipe (Fig 9) modified with an inner sleeve and plain-top, respectively (Fig 10). This was called 'improved draughting' because the changes enabled the engines to steam more freely, even with inferior fuel.

The jumper-top, unless carefully looked after was liable, due to carbon deposits, to stick in its upper position, or even to stick partially raised, and then the engine would not steam properly. When regular maintenance ceased to be feasible, this characteristic became a menace to locomotive reliability, so jumper-tops (or caps) were abandoned.

The first pattern of self-cleaning smokebox was also fitted (Figs 11, 12). This followed similar experiments on the London Midland Region in an effort to reduce the turnround time at depots. The smokebox baffles and mesh plates were arranged so that the blast from the fire came through the tubes into the smokebox, taking the ashes on through the mesh plates and up the chimney into the atmosphere. This prevented any build-up of the ash in the bottom of the smokebox. The whole class received these modifications before the introduction of the double chimney.

The most far-reaching and significant changes in *King* design since their introduction began in 1953 with 'controlled road tests'; 6001 *King Edward VII* hauling twenty-five coaches from Reading to Stoke Gifford and back. Soon afterwards, modified outside steam pipes of larger radius began to make their appearance (Fig 8) following occasional fractures of the original pattern.

Although 6014 was fitted with a cab roof ventilator in 1935, when streamlined, it was not until 1954 that this modification was made to the rest of the *King* class (Fig 13).

In September 1955 *King Richard III* was the first *King* to be fitted with a double chimney. The chimney casing was a fabricated type (Fig 12) and fourteen other *King*s were also so fitted. Back pressure in the blast pipe was an important factor in the limiting of locomotive performance and, therefore, the larger the area of cross-section of the blastpipe, the less coal would be burnt and more power developed at high speeds. So, fitting a double chimney enabled two blastpipes to have a much greater area of cross section, taken together, than a single blastpipe, to produce the maximum of steam from the boiler. Hence double chimneys meant higher speeds available and more steam produced from the same boiler.

No 6000 *King George V* received a single chimney with a larger diameter. Only 6003 *King George IV* and 6020 *King Henry IV* were similarly fitted (Fig 11). Later, all three

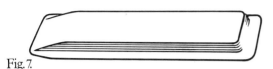

Fig. 7.

Box cover housing the lubricating pipes to valves, pistons and regulator valve as they leave the boiler casing and enter the smokebox.
Version as on 6022 when first fitted with four-row superheater.

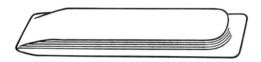

Standard version of box cover housing the lubricating pipes on four-row superheater engines.
Oil supply was dependent on regulator position. An OIL/NO OIL gauge was provided in the cab.

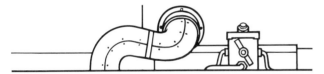

Fig. 8.

Final standard position of mechanical lubricator. Modified outside steam pipe, following occasional fractures of original.

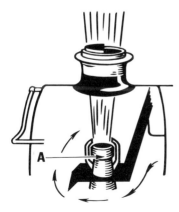

Fig. 9.

Original chimney with capuchon. The blastpipe had a 'jumper' top (A) which moved upwards to give a wider opening when working hard.

Fig. 10.

Modified with sleeve fitted inside the original chimney, first fitted in 1952 to 6001. First the 'jumper' top was wedged down, then a plain-top blastpipe substituted and self-cleaning smokebox followed.
Numerous variations, following many experiments, occurred from 1953 until 1956, when double chimneys were finally fitted to the entire class.

Fig. 11.

Wide diameter chimney with early form of self-cleaning smokebox first fitted on locomotives 6000/6003/6020 in 1955-56.

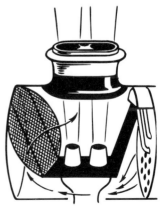

Fig. 12.

First built-up double chimney and double blastpipe with self-cleaning smokebox.
Arrows show path of ash and gases being drawn through the wire mesh before going up the chimney.

locomotives received standard double chimneys.

A small modification appeared in the front framing on some *King*s with the fitting of a strengthening piece surrounding the lifting holes (Fig 4).

Following the findings of an investigation into the derailment of 4-6-2-2 locomotive No 60700 on the Eastern Region in September 1955, all *King*s were temporarily withdrawn from service on 28 January 1956. The investigation had shown defects in welding repairs to the bogie of No 60700, and it was found that several *King*s had also developed fatigue cracks. During the next few weeks reinforcing bars were welded on all bogie frames at critical positions (Fig 14).

From 1956 onwards the *King*s were virtually new engines, receiving new boilers and new inside cylinders, and with new front end framing welded to the original rear section. They were also fitted with standard cast-iron double chimneys. Clearly, these were of North Eastern origin (Fig 15) and expressed the design influence of the aforementioned R.A. Smeddle.

The self-cleaning arrangement in the smokebox was replaced in 1958 with a basket-type spark arrester surrounding the double blastpipe (Fig 15).

In the late 1950s a few *King*s were fitted with a new type of valve spindle cover (Fig 16B) replacing the earlier version (Fig 16A).

In 1959 a new type buffer (Fig 17) began to replace the tapered type (Fig 18). 6000 *King George V* was fitted with a temporary middle lamp bracket (Fig 18) some time during 1957, and a wooden plinth appeared beneath the famous bell about 1960 (Fig 17).

This was virtually the end of *King* class developments and they were withdrawn from service in 1962. All in all, the *King*s were a most successful class of locomotive, trouble free, reliable, and able to handle satisfactorily and efficiently the heaviest trains on the Western Region.

From the driver's point of view the *King*s were excellent engines, always seeming to have power and speed in hand, and 'keeping their feet' remarkably well due to the 67½ tons on the coupled wheels. From the fireman's point of view they were free-steaming, but, especially with the double chimney, there was a tendency for coal to be burned more rapidly at the front of the grate, making it really hard work when the coal was powdery and when watered turned into a wet sludge which would not leave the shovel.

There are innumerable recorded instances of the combination of load hauling and speed by *King*s, and perhaps the most interesting is the performance of No 6001 *King Edward VII* on a test run with a load of 798 tons, when the speed up the long steady drag from Didcot to Swindon was held at only just under 60 mph.

Research and diagrammatic drawings by Richard S. Potts.

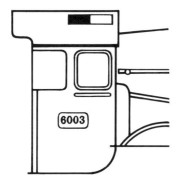

Fig. 13.

Standard cab with addition of roof ventilator slide.

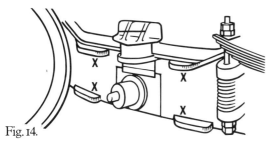

Fig. 14.

Strengthening pieces (X) welded to bogie frame plates.

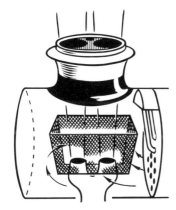

Fig. 15.

Standard cast-iron double chimney. With double blastpipe, first fitted with self-cleaning smokebox as in Fig 12. Eventually all *King*s received a wire-mesh cage surrounding the blastpipe and connecting at the top with the bottom of the chimney petticoat (omitted for simplicity from the drawing).

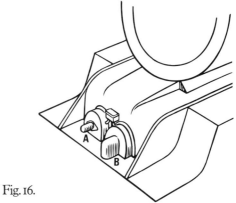

Fig. 16.

(A) Original valve spindle cover.
(B) Valve spindle covers on 6020-29 when built.

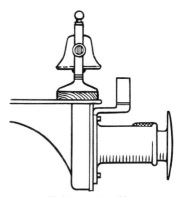

Fig. 17.

Final pattern parallel barrel buffers.
Wooden plinth fitted beneath bell on 6000.
Original and final position of centre lamp bracket on 6000.

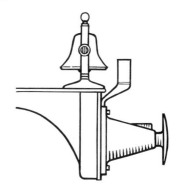

Fig. 18.

Original tapering barrel buffers.
Original bell position on 6000.
Temporary lamp bracket on 6000, about 1957.

## Simplified List of Modifications

| YEAR | ENGINE | MODIFICATION |
|------|--------|--------------|
| 1947 | 6022 | Four row superheater, mechanical lubricator. |
| 1948 | 6009/6025 | Experimental dark blue livery. |
| | | Red, cream and grey lining. |
| | — | Square edge step to top of inside valve casing. |
| 1949 | — | Start to gradual introduction of four row superheaters. |
| 1950 | — | Standard Caledonian blue livery. |
| | | Black and white lining. |
| 1952 | 6001/6017 | 'Sleeved' chimney (improved draughting). |
| | | Self-cleaning smokebox. |
| | — | Reintroduction of Brunswick green. |
| 1953 | 6001 | Controlled road test: Reading to Stoke Gifford, |
| | | Twenty-five coaches. Modified outside steampipes. |
| 1954 | — | Roof ventilators become standard. |
| 1955 | 6000 | Large diameter single chimney (6003/20 also fitted). |
| | 6015 | First double chimney (fabricated) and double blastpipe (fourteen locos). |
| 1956 | — | Whole class withdrawn temporarily. Bogie repairs. |
| | 6004 | First standard cast-iron double chimney, NER design. |
| 1958 | — | Basket type spark arresters. |
| 1959 | — | New pattern buffers. |
| 1960 | 6000 | Wooden plinth beneath bell. |
| 1962 | — | Whole class withdrawn from service. |

Acknowledgements
RCTS, *Locomotives of the GWR* and *The Railway Observer*
O.S. Nock, *The GWR Stars, Castles & Kings. Part Two.*

# Footplate Experiences

When the Great Western Railway introduced the *King* class locomotive in 1927 it was proclaimed as the most powerful engine operating on any British railway. Although derided by some critics as little more than an enlarged *Castle*, the *King*s were soon winning their laurels in regular service, particularly on the stiff banks and gradients of the West Country. Such was the excellence of C.B.Collett's design that the *King*s ran for more than twenty years without major modification. But post-war, and after nationalisation, a series of important modifications were carried out in an endeavour to make the *King*s run faster, or pull heavier loads than in their original form, or to make steam on poorer coal.

In the photographs that appear later each *King* locomotive is shown in its original form with single chimney, and as it appeared in later years on British Railways fitted with a double chimney. Each photograph illustrates a particular modification or design feature. Selection has involved much searching discussion, it being extremely difficult to decide which pair of photographs to choose from so many hundreds for each of the thirty *King*s. Certainly they represent the cream of Kenneth Leech's unique collection.

The manner in which these photographs were taken was unusual. Such was the rapport between photographer and enginemen that the locomotives were 'posed' at Chippenham, Bath, Bristol, and other main line stations, and at Swindon engines were placed in positions outside the works so that Kenneth Leech could photograph them.

No layman could have had a closer involvement with steam engines than Kenneth Leech. On the footplate he proved himself a first-class fireman and driver, respected by enginemen and locomotive inspectors alike. He says he liked firing because it was a man's job and needed skill and judgement, and a 'knack'. And driving, especially stopping at platforms, meant apprehension, as well as enjoyment.

In his 'retirement' he has travelled some 45,000 miles on the footplate, usually as fireman or driver. This activity spanned fifteen years or so, when he was making not only a catalogue of the *King*'s mechanical modifications, but unwittingly compiling an important photographic record of the enginemen who handled them, and with whom he worked with mutual respect and understanding. In the annals of railway history there can be no parallel. Kenneth Leech, the man and his photographs, have a fascinating story to tell; one which can never be repeated or surpassed now that steam traction has been withdrawn from British Railways.

## Some Footplate Trips

It is logical in any account of steam locomotive classes to begin with the first engine built, but in the case of No 6000 *King George V* it is imperative. She is by far the best known of the royal thirty, having travelled across the Atlantic to North America in 1927. The medals mounted on the side of the engine cab over the number plate and the large brass bell on her buffer beam are mementoes of her historic appearance at the Baltimore & Ohio Railway Company's Centenary Exhibition.

Kenneth Leech's first trip on this locomotive was in 1954 on a running-in turn, when she was fresh out of Swindon Works after repair. He rode on her on many occasions and always found her a very good engine, but no better than many others. She had a very distinctive characteristic in the way she rode: from time to time, at speed, she would come down with a hard bump and a crash. He never experienced this on any other *King*, but it was well-known that No 6000 was sensitive to rail irregularities.

He recalls a run on *King George V* from Paddington to Plymouth on the '10.30 Limited' with a relatively light train of about 350 tons: she simply played with it all the way. It was as well she had a margin of power and speed, for after passing through Reading on schedule they were pulled up at Theale where a cow had strayed onto the line, and lost ten minutes. Going up both Dainton and Rattray banks it was 40 per cent cut-off and full regulator, and time was made up without ever exceeding 90 mph. Even after being checked by a signal outside Plymouth they still ran into North Road station a few minutes early.

But *King George V* was not always in such good form and Kenneth's last trip on her just before diesels took over, was a miserable business. He drove her from Bath to Chippenham, but she had been sadly neglected and was not steaming at all well. He could not even get her going fast enough to make a rush at Box Tunnel and only just managed to crawl out at the top end at 15-20 mph. Poor-steaming *King*s were the exception and Kenneth recalls only one that was consistently less good than the rest when he was firing her: No 6026. But in his experience *King*s were a very level lot with No 6016 and No 6019 marginally the best.

One day he rode from Bath to Chippenham on the 'Warship' diesel, D800, and noticed that the driver had put her in the last notch for maximum power as soon as the permitted speed to do so had been reached, and kept it so right on to Thingley. He noted on paper the times and speeds at various points and within a day or two, when on the same job with No 6019, he told the driver about D800. As hoped, the driver took this as a challenge and No 6019 easily beat the diesel's performance, running at over 60 mph through Box Tunnel on an up-grade of 1 in 100, with 280 tons behind the tender.

His most exciting run on a *King* was on the down 'Bristolian' with No

6015 *King Richard III* soon after she had been fitted with a double chimney. It was her driver's last week before retiring and he had asked Kenneth to accompany him. Sure enough there were fireworks: 68 mph at West Ealing; 72mph at Southall; 77mph at Hayes, increasing to 83mph at West Drayton. There was a 3½ minutes stop at Slough for signals, then rapid acceleration up to 78mph at Maidenhead; 84mph at Twyford, where the 'S' curve speed restriction of 75mph went by the board. 'Very rough indeed around curves at Twyford', read Kenneth's notes.

The best was yet to come. Through Goring at 88mph, and holding 90mph at Cholsey, after a slight adverse gradient. It was later confirmed that it was the greatest horsepower recorded in service by a *King* at anything like that speed. The cut-off reading was 20 per cent; regulator was half open; boiler pressure 245 lb/in², and water gauge reading half full, which shows that the engine was not being driven beyond its continuous limit.

After a signal check at Didcot and a 15mph restriction at Lockinge, there was an acceleration to 84mph, and at the foot of Wootton Bassett Bank speed was 105mph. Four miles on at Avon Bridge it was still an almost incredible 98mph. But even so, after further signal checks the train ran 10 minutes late into Bristol. The ATC cab signalling had not been working properly and had given a warning siren at every signal, on or off, all the way. Kenneth had also smelt sizzling oil as they went through Bath Station, but thought it was the oil on piston rods or valve spindles being cooked. Not so: it was the left-hand leading axle box running very hot, and at journey's end it was almost welded to the axle. In trying to remove it the Bath Road fitters drilled through into the axle and scrapped a practically new crank axle. The engine had to go into Swindon Works for major surgery. A sad end to a glorious run.

An unforgettable out-and-home journey was a run down to Plymouth on No 6012 with a normal express train, making a few stops. Glorious weather all the way, an engine in tip-top order, smooth, responsive and steaming beautifully; and over eighty photographs taken from the footplate. On the return journey No 6012 was literally cruising home on 12 per cent cut-off practically all the way from Newton Abbot, but at Westbury the fireman struck a patch of bad coal in the tender, and the pressure gauge reading began to drop back. The coal was small and full of dust, forming a clinging, paste-like substance on the shovel. In the firebox it either went straight up the chimney, or else ran back onto the firebars as clinker. Luckily, the fireman soon dug into better coal, and No 6012 got back into her stride and made up the few minutes lost through poor steaming.

But just to show the vagaries of steam engines, there was another, earlier occasion when No 6012 told a different story. She was on the '10.30 Limited' Paddington to Plymouth, and from the outset it was clear she was not going to steam. The pressure gauge needle never got past the 150 lb/in² mark, and with the water level showing just around the bottom nut in the glass a message was thrown out to a signal box asking the Reading pilot to stand-by. Reading pilots were known all over the system as being very rough engines and No 4960 *Pyle Hall* was no exception. The driver took her up to 77mph, but the inspector riding with him became nervous and would not again go beyond 70mph. Rough engines could be exciting, but they were tiring on legs and ears because the footplate was unsteady and a series of crashes accompanied all the rail joints.

The cause of No 6012s bad steaming was later diagnosed as a baffle plate that had slid forward, partially covering the blast pipe. It was a very dangerous fault: if it had covered the blast pipe completely there would almost certainly have been a blow-back of fire into the cab. This plate was always removed when the boiler was washed-out and it had not been clipped back in the smoke box, where its purpose was to baffle spark throwing. Had it been known what the trouble was at the time, the plate could quite easily have been pushed back with a shovel, then clipped into position. There would not have been any need for No 4960, and Kenneth would not have enjoyed his unexpected ride.

Poor quality coal was usually the cause of bad steaming, particularly if the tender had been loaded, as was often the case, with a mixture of small coal, dust and ovoids. The trouble was that knobs or ovoids would roll down easily to the front of the grate, but the small coal would not. Also, it prevented the ovoids from rolling so that they tended to get caught up in the backward draught of the engine blast, towards the top of the brick arch. It was as though a gale was blowing against the fireman, lifting the coal as it came off the shovel and making his task more arduous, particularly if the engine was being worked hard.

### Firing Practice
Firing a *King* was a man's job. This was because these engines burned more coal in the front of the firebox than they did under the firehole, which meant that the fireman did not follow the usual Great Western practice of packing coal right up to or above firehole level, into the corners, leaving the fire thin at the front. When firing a double chimney *King,* the greater part of the coal had to be thrown the full length of the firebox, a distance of 11ft preferably right to the front, so that it actually knocked on the tube plate.

If the coals were allowed to build-up under the brick arch, starving the fire in the front part of the grate, the pressure gauge needle would

*'The Merchant Venturer',*
*headed by a* King, *passing*
*through Chippenham.*

suddenly fall back as the engine stopped steaming. A good fireman would, therefore, watch the surface of the fire from back to front the whole time. This was easier to do when soft Welsh coal was being burned than if hard Yorkshire was used, the glare from the surface of the fire being appreciably less with soft coal.

One point of interest about Great Western firing practice, which railwaymen from other regions always thought an unnecessary waste of energy, was the technique of lifting up the firehole flap between each shovelful of coal. This singular action probably accounted for the large, rather clumsy, Great Western shovel, for with its capacity to carry 18-20 lb of coal, it was worth taking time and trouble to pack it properly. By comparison, the smaller LNER shovel was a weapon of precision with which the fireman could take a 'pepper spoonful' of coal and point it exactly where he wanted it in the firebox.

It was almost universal on the Great Western that the firehole flap, an extremely light iron casting, raised by a chain at the side and hinged at the bottom, would be normally left raised. When the fireman had got his shovel filled and ready, he would yank the chain with his left hand and the flap would fall down. Then, after he had fired the shovelful, up his left hand would go, yanking the chain and lifting the flap back into position. He would take his time about gathering more coal, digging back into the tender, maybe breaking up a large lump, but all the while the flap would be in the up position. This method of firing produced the hottest fire and, by not having the firehole door open more than was necessary, the possibility of cold air entering the firebox and causing leaking tubes and, perhaps, broken stays was reduced. Once an engine was steaming freely it would be run with dampers partly closed and flap up, so as to maintain the proper balance of air below and above the grate.

### Drivers and Driving

It was surprising the way in which top-link drivers would vary their way of working a *King* over the same route with the same weight of train. Kenneth Leech recalls in particular Driver Walter Harris, a great character and a first-class engineman who, when working between Newton Abbot and Plymouth on the down '10.30 Limited' was continually altering the setting of the reversing lever to suit the road. Up the steep banks of Dainton and Rattery he would work the engine at 40-45 per cent cut-off, dropping down to 15 per cent on the easy portions of the road. But when he shut off going down banks, or because of a curve ahead with perhaps a 50mph speed limit, the reversing lever would be dropped into its 'rolling' position of 40 per cent cut-off. Driver Harris's mates thought him one of the greatest drivers on the Great Western. He certainly saved the company a good deal of coal!

On the other hand another of Kenneth's driver friends working the same weight of train over the exact route would simply set the reversing lever in 40 per cent and give the engine full regulator up the banks, pull it back into first port on the level and shut it off downhill. Always the lever was notched up in 40 per cent. The driver simply altered the regulator from full open to completely shut according to the gradient and the circumstances. He may have saved himself trouble, but he was not popular with his fireman!

Many drivers were really first class, skilled men who 'felt' their engine and found the best way to drive it in the first mile or two. Others had a set pattern and drove every engine the same; theirs was a rough and ready approximation which enabled them to get along but did not permit development of maximum power or minimum coal consumption. No real thought went into the driving. The job had become a routine, and while they drove with due regard for safety and good time-keeping they were not in tune with their engine.

The good driver was a thinking man, always prepared to match his wits against his engine's performance. The skill of such men was intuitive. One such man was Bert Potter, a *Royal* driver at Old Oak Common, who was on No 6015 with the '10.30 Limited' when she made her maximum speed of 110mph. After this epic run Kenneth Leech asked Bert Potter what his cut-off had been and he replied that he hadn't the slightest idea! He said he had simply 'dropped it a little bit and let it find its own position'. Then he had just checked it when, on its own, it had tended to go a bit too far!

Kenneth Leech was known and respected as being a driver of no mean ability. It was said of him that he was able to get on an unfamiliar engine and within half a mile he would have found the best way to drive it. Driver Charlie Wasley was one who had a great respect for his ability, and on the occasions that Kenneth drove his engine Charlie would stand with his back to him, leaning on the water tender pick-up handle, so showing his absolute confidence in his unofficial workmate. Kenneth always maintained that no two engines were exactly alike and always tried to ascertain their peculiarities, and drive in the best way possible.

Another first-class driver with whom he rode hundreds of miles was Charlie Brown, a short, compact man, who in his younger days had been one of the top-link firemen working on record-breaking trips with *Castle*s on the 'Cheltenham Flyer'. He must really have packed a punch on the shovel. It was Charlie Brown who proved to Kenneth that when a *King* was driven really hard it was beyond him physically. It was with No 6013, on an up train from Bristol, and Kenneth managed perfectly well in the early stages, but from Box onwards, when Charlie Brown really put pressure on, Kenneth was unable to

get the coal on quickly enough and had to hand over to the regular fireman. 'I think Charlie Brown was rather tickled at the thought of being able to beat me', chuckled Kenneth.

A professional fireman would maintain a firing rate of 70-80 lb of coal per minute for long periods, and at the age of sixty-eight Kenneth Leech was still able to average 60 lb per minute for about forty minutes. It was his rule never to give up if he could possibly help it, and on one occasion his driver remarked, after he had been firing continuously for a long period: 'You'll never die, they'll have to shoot you!'

Due to the slow speed, working hard up a steep bank was not as tiring as might be expected, but gradients taken at 60mph were the hardest and made the fireman sweat. There was always a chance of relaxing down the other side and then the engine would seem to be enjoying it and the driver would be happy. And the fireman? He most certainly would be enjoying a respite from labouring on the shovel!

One evening, on the running-in turn from Swindon, No 6014 arrived with a driver whom Kenneth knew, and he was allowed to drive the train from Bath to Chippenham. It was scheduled to stop at every station, but the regulator was so stiff that it would not open past the first port once the engine was in motion, so that time was being lost. They stopped at Mill Lane just at the entrance to the lower end of Box Tunnel (the west end) already several minutes late, and Kenneth decided that No 6014 must have a bit more than first port on the regulator. The rail was perfectly dry, so there seemed a good chance that the engine would not slip if the regulator was opened fully when the 'right away' was given. But he was wrong!

He gave the regulator an almighty jerk, and the engine roared off in a terrific slip, luckily just moving forward enough not to grind the rails. The regulator was stuck firm and would not budge. So Kenneth tried to reverse the engine by putting it up into mid-gear, but the gear reverser was so stiff it could not be moved. And so, with No 6014 roaring her head off the only thing to do was to apply the brakes and prevent the driving wheels from spinning. Eventually, Kenneth was able to shut the regulator and have another try, deciding that he would need to go very steadily and lose time if necessary.

Next day, the driver told him that when they had got to Swindon the guard had come up to him and asked: 'What happened at Mill Lane, Fred?' And he had replied: 'Oh, we got off the road just for a moment or two, but got on again all right on our own, and there was no trouble after that!'

*6012* King Edward VI *approaching Teignmouth.*

The normal method for opening the regulator fully when stiff was to pull the engine up to mid-gear so that very little steam was taken and the pressure on the back of the slide valve of the regulator would not be so different from the pressure below it. The reason why this would not work when No 6014 was at Mill Lane was because the train was on a gradient of 1 in 100, and would almost certainly have stopped dead had this procedure taken place while it was still moving slowly. It might have even rolled backwards.

Although No 6014s trip was unfortunate, it proved yet again that there was always something unexpected likely to happen with a steam engine. It was one very good reason for keeping one's attention inside the engine, but Kenneth admits that when not driving he enjoyed leaning out of the cab side and watching the crosshead of the outside left cylinder flashing backwards and forwards, always seeming to be doing it rapidly and yet deliberately: a mixture of fast and slow.

The enginemen knew their road from beginning to end, including local names of level crossings and farms and of course they knew exactly where they would come in sight of each signal. But there were few who had their attention drawn away from the footplate to the scenery outside for more than a few seconds. After all they were doing a job, a job that they had to be right on top of or there could be catastrophic results. Moreover, it was a job normally carried on with much accompanying noise and distraction, requiring continuous concentration.

On one occasion Kenneth was driving No 6012 on a down express through Box Tunnel, when to his great surprise she came out after two miles down a gradient of 1 in 100 at a lower speed than she went in. The brakes had been dragging, but in the darkness it was impossible to see the vacuum gauge. The brakes were soon blown-off and they went on to make up the time before the next stop, but Kenneth was still a little worried: had someone pulled the communication cord and made a light application of the brake by that means? The regular driver was not in the least concerned, knowing that the pulling of the cord would have caused a much more severe brake application, and would have stopped the train. But the experience shows how alert a driver needed to be, not only to what was going on at the lineside and at the signals, but also as to the little details in the cab.

On another *King*, half way through Box Tunnel, Kenneth saw a red light approaching on the down side. 'Red light!', he yelled out, and applied the brake. It was not until he had almost pulled up the train that he discovered it was the Chippenham shunting engine going to Bath, and that the fireman had failed to remove the red slide from what had been his tail lamp and what was then his head lamp. Yet another illustration of keeping alert while driving. No wonder, after eight hours on the job, drivers came-off shift mentally fatigued.

## Speed and Power

Weight for weight, the *King*s were the most powerful engines in Britain, but they were not so big or heavy as the later LNER and LMS Pacifics, which were more able to sustain their extra power over longer runs, or with inferior coal.

The only engines against which Kenneth could personally compare *King*s were the LNER Pacifics of the A1, A3 and A4 classes. He always felt that a *King* was rather better than an A3; perhaps not quite so good as an A4 — but very little in it, except that the A4 was generally freer-running. The speed at which a *King* seemed to run freely was just below 90mph (say, 88), whereas an A4 seemed freer at just above 90mph (say, 92), but this was over a few trips only and other A4s might have given him a different idea. However, there was no question at all, the A1 was definitely more powerful than a *King*.

As one driver remarked to Kenneth when he was showing him what an A1 could do with the 'Flying Scotsman' up Stoke Bank: 'I could kill any fireman with one of these!'

Nearly all the *King*s Kenneth rode on had four-row superheaters and were fitted with double chimneys. It was only at the beginning, when he had no standard of comparison for them that the engines had single chimneys. There was no question at all: the double chimney was a great improvement. It made for a much freer-running engine, and the degree to which it did so was surprising even to the Swindon test staff under Mr S.O. Ell. It was Ell who commented to Kenneth Leech how delighted he was, and how much better No 6015 was with a double chimney.

One thing missing from the Great Western *King*s was the comfort of the seats on the LNER Pacifics where, instead of having a hard board to sit on there was a cushion seat, which made all the difference on a long run. After a trip from Paddington to Plymouth on No 6000 with the '10.30 Limited', first stop Plymouth, Kenneth returned on No 6027 and, feeling rather weary after 300 miles or thereabouts, he sat down on the cab seat for some part of the way. He says he was rather wishful of taking his meals from the mantel-piece for the next two days; so sore and stiff was he from having ridden the Great Western's hard board seat!

The opening years of the 1960s saw the end of the *King*s, as they were gradually replaced by the diesels. It seemed ironic that the strongest, speediest, and possibly the most handsome of the old Great Western's locomotive classes was the first to go to the scrapyard. The first *King*s to be broken-up were undoubtedly in need of very heavy repairs, but the last of the class were simply withdrawn because there was work for them only if the diesels were laid aside temporarily.

# Taking photographs...

In these days, when photographic retailers display a plethora of super-de-luxe cameras and multifarious accessories, it is interesting that Kenneth Leech took these superb photographs with an unknown make of camera.

He described it as: 'A 120 folding camera of German origin (manufacturers name illegible on camera) with a F3.5 lens and Compur Rapid shutter, giving me a 1/400″ sec exposure, which I 'helped' by panning the camera at half train speed.'

He used HPS Ilford film (no longer made) for the majority of his pictures, and MicrodolX developers at 80°F; 10°F higher than specified. Kenneth believed this higher temperature improved picture content without increasing grain size. He wanted brightness, sharpness and detail of shadow in all his negatives.

The camera was very light and simple. On rock climbs, when photographing fellow climbers, it could be held in one hand with an eye to the viewfinder and the shutter released while the other hand was occupied holding onto the rock.

# ...from the footplate

When photographing from the moving locomotive footplate, he reckoned to press the shutter release *between* passing over rail joints, leaning well out of the cab and focussing on infinity.

On one trip with No 5082 on the Cumbrian Coast Express he used a rock-climbing sling around the water pick-up column to get further out and have both hands free. But this was not popular with the crew or the Inspector — even though Kenneth explained he was trying to get the connecting rod and, if possible, the coupling rods, too!

# Portraits of 'Kings'

## — as built and with final modifications

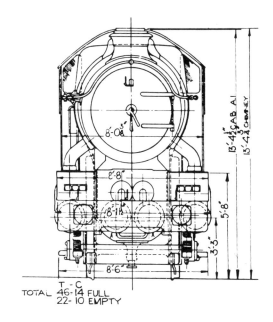

8-0⅜"

8'-8"

8-1½"

8-6"

13'-4½" CAB AI
13'-4¾" CHIMNEY

5'-8"

3'-3"

T - C
TOTAL 46-14 FULL
22-10 EMPTY

ENGINE & TENDER  T - C
TOTAL  WEIGHT FULL 135·14

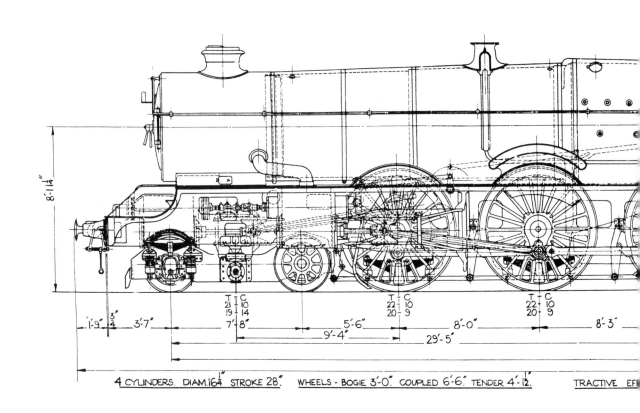

8'-11¼"

T   C          T   C          T   C
21   10        22   10        22   10
19   14        20   9         20   9

1'-9¾"  3'-7"      7'-8"        5'-6"       8'-0"        8'-3"
                         9'-4"
                              29'-5"

4 CYLINDERS. DIAM. 16¼" STROKE 28".   WHEELS - BOGIE 3'-0". COUPLED 6'-6". TENDER 4'-1½".      TRACTIVE EF

# 'King' (6000) Class
# Four Cylinder 4-6-0 Type
(Introduced 1927)

Designed by C.B. Collett, the 'Kings' were the most powerful passenger locomotives in Great Britain. They were introduced to handle heavy traffic and fast running schedules, particularly over the steep gradients of the West Country main line on such trains as the 'Cornish Riviera Limited'.

| | |
|---|---|
| Cylinders: | Four<br>Diam 16¼in<br>Stroke 28in |
| Boiler: | Barrel 16ft 0in<br>Diam } 5ft 6¼in<br>Outs } 6ft 0in |

| | |
|---|---|
| Firebox: | Length Outs 11ft 6in |
| Heating Surface: | 2490 sq ft |
| Area of Firegrate: | 34.2 sq ft |
| Wheels: | Bogie 3ft 0in<br>Coupled 6ft 6in |
| Water Capacity of Tender: | 4000 gallons |
| Working Pressure: | 250lbs |
| Tractive Effort: | 40,300lbs |
| Total Weight of Tender: | 46 tons 14cwt Full<br>22 tons 10cwt Empty |
| Total Weight of Engine: | 89 tons 0cwt Full<br>81 tons 10cwt Empty |

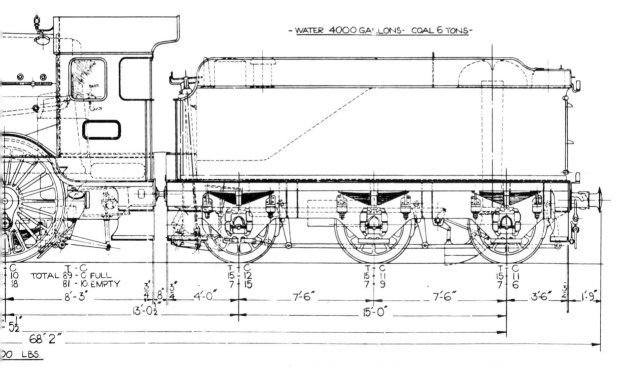

- WATER 4000 GALLONS · COAL 6 TONS -

(DRAWINGS BY COURTESY BRITISH RAIL)

*Clearing smokebox char.
Performed alongside the
coaling stage, it was a
familiar sight before
introduction of the self-
cleaning smokebox in
1952 (Engine Modifica-
tions).
(Photo: British Rail)*

*Boiler washing out. Note
baffle plate on right hand
buffer beam. Kenneth
Leech refers to a failure
with No 6012 (Footplate
Experiences) when the
baffle plate had not been
clipped back in position,
causing the engine to
steam badly.
(Photo: British Rail)*

*Opposite:
Cab Layout No 6000
'King George V'
(Photo: British Rail)*

# 6000
# King George V

*Built: June 1927*
*Withdrawn: December 1962*
*Mileage: 1,910,424*
*Disposal: Leased by BR to H.P.Bulmers Ltd. Preserved in running order at Bulmer Railway Centre, Hereford*

*At Chippenham, 29 April 1954, fresh out of Swindon Works. 6000 clearly displays inner sleeved chimney and modified outside steam pipes with mechanical lubricator in the rear position. Other modifications include stepped inside cylinder cover and cab roof ventilator.*

'This photograph was taken on the day, but not on the train, on which I had my first trip on 6000, which was from Bath to Chippenham.
'She needed firing to the front of the firebox and threw a lot of fire from the chimney on this occasion, due, of course, to the improved draughting of the sleeved chimney and smaller blast pipe orifice.'

'6000 steamed well on nine out of the ten trips I had on her footplate, whether fitted with single or double chimney. It

*Standing in Bristol Temple Meads, 5 June 1959, the engine presents quite a different appearance as fitted with a standard cast double chimney. Mechanical lubricator has been moved to its final position and strengthening pieces welded to the bogie frame plates. Deep covers to inside valve spindles (first introduced on Nos 6020-9). Bell mounted on a wooden plinth and updated BR insignia on tender.*

was almost certainly neglect which caused her to steam badly on the one exceptional occasion, for she had been steaming well on coal which I described as rubbish only three weeks previously.'

*The brass bell on the front footplating and the two cabside medallions are mementoes of 6000's visit to the USA in 1927 for the Baltimore & Ohio Railroad centenary celebrations.*

# 6001
# King Edward VII

*Built: July 1927*
*Withdrawn: September 1962*
*Mileage: 1,941,044*
*Disposal: Cox & Danks Ltd*

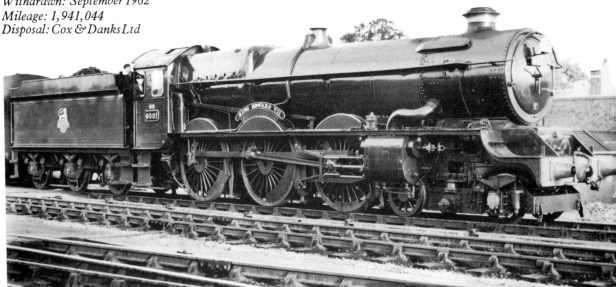

*At Chippenham, 1 October 1954, with sleeved chimney fitted to four-row superheated boiler. Modified outside steam pipes with mechanical lubricator in rear position. Inside cylinder cover step and cab roof ventilator, Original tapered-barrel buffers.*

*6001 was used on steam trials in 1953, eventually hauling a test train of twenty-five coaches from Reading to Stoke Gifford and back.*

'On this occasion (1 October 1954) I drove 6001 but found her "sluggish". Perhaps in more experienced hands she might have seemed a different engine. She was new out of shops after repair and may have been "tight", as the phrase was. It must be understood that in all cases of footplate riding, the driver was present and no doubt fully alert to his duties, while permitting my actions as his deputy.'

*Summer 1958, at Chippenham on a running-in turn. Now fitted with a cast double chimney, mechanical lubricator in forward position, strengthened bogie frame and parallel-barrel buffers.*

## 6002
## King William IV

*Built: July 1927*
*Withdrawn: September 1962*
*Mileage: 1,891,952*
*Disposal: Cox & Danks Ltd*

*At Bath, 17 December 1954, fitted with a sleeved chimney on an old two-row superheated boiler. Modified outside steam pipes, but has not yet received a mechanical lubricator. Third boiler band joining bracket visible, rather unusual.*

'One of my trips on 6002 was an unlucky one. I fired confidently, but I could not get the rather poor coal to the front of the firebox and she would not steam. I found out too late that the deflector plate in the fire-hole had sagged downwards towards its tip quite seriously. Usually one cures this fault by wedging a small piece of coal between the top of the deflector plate and the fire-hole ring, so that the front end of the plate is cocked upwards, and all is well thereafter.'

*Bath, 3 March 1956, soon after receiving a new four-row superheated boiler. Note built-up type of double chimney. Cast iron plate 'SC' beneath shed code denotes self-cleaning smokebox. Mechanical lubricator is in final position forward of outside steam pipes.*

# 6003
# King George IV

*Built: July 1927*
*Withdrawn: June 1962*
*Mileage: 1,920,479*
*Disposal: Swindon*

*In Swindon Works yard,
31 January 1954, after
overhaul. Fitted with a
sleeved chimney, four-row
superheated boiler, and
mechanical lubricator is
behind the modified outside
steam pipes.*

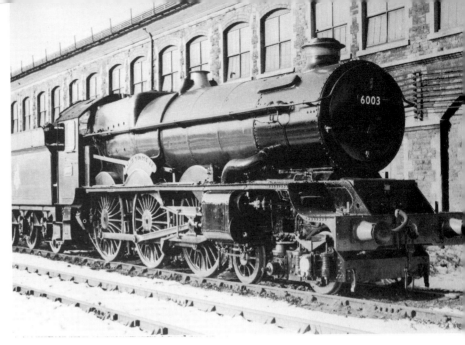

'My diary records that I drove 6003 on 13 September 1958 down to
Bath, but that the young fireman could not make her steam well. On
the return trip I fired from Bristol Temple Meads to Bath, and did all
right! No doubt the fire had been cleaned at Bristol.'

*6003* King George IV *with the up test run for
the 'Bristolian' 30 April 1954. At Hullavington.
speed 87 mph. Full regulator. 15 per cent cut-off.*

*Chippenham, 31 July 1958, fresh out of Swindon Works. Standard double chimney; mechanical lubricator in forward position and strengthened bogie frame.*

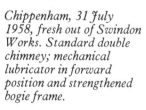

# 6004
# King George III

*Built: July 1927*
*Withdrawn: June 1962*
*Mileage: 1,917,258*
*Disposal: Swindon*

'This photograph was taken from the carriage window of a train passing the Works at about 60 mph.'

*Outside Swindon Works,*
*8 September 1953, fitted*
*with sleeved chimney and*
*four-row superheated boiler.*

'Standing beside the loco is the late Stanley Morris, a foreman at the Works and my very good friend. He used to pose engines in mint condition at the Works for me to photograph at weekends.'

*Another Swindon portrait, 18 November 1956. Standard double chimney; mechanical lubricator in forward position; stepped* *inside cylinder covers. Bogie frames have been strengthened and cab roof ventilators fitted. The engine is attached to a temporary tender.*

# 6005
# King George II

*Built: July 1927*
*Withdrawn: November 1962*
*Mileage: 1,679,275*
*Disposal: J. Cashmore Ltd*

*Swindon, 30 January 1955, fresh from 'A' shop. Sleeved chimney with four-row superheated boiler; mechanical lubricator set forward of modified outside steam pipes, stepped inside cylinder cover, deep spindle covers, and cab roof ventilators.*

'In February 1955 I rode up from Bath on her; she rode nicely but with just a sensation that she would soon become a bit "gay"; that is the expression then used to describe an engine riding in a lively manner, but not really rough.'

*Standing at Chippenham, May 1962, with Driver Colin (Con) Mason, of Swindon. Fitted with standard double chimney, parallel-barrel buffers and strengthened bogie frame.*

'My first acquaintance with Con Mason was when I photographed him on a *Castle* at Chippenham, a distraction which caused him to leave an oil-bottle on the front end of the footplate. He found it still there when he went round the engine again at Bristol, a tribute both to the good riding of the engine and to the excellence of the permanent way.'

# 6006
# King George I

*Built: February 1928*
*Withdrawn: February 1962*
*Mileage: 1,593,367*
*Disposal: Swindon*

*At Chippenham in 1952. The keen-eyed observer will have noted that 6006 is in the short-lived BR blue livery, lined out in black and white. Otherwise, the locomotive is in almost original condition, She has yet to receive a mechanical lubricator, modified outside steam pipes, cab roof ventilator, or any form of new pattern chimney, as a consequence of experiments into improved draughting.*

'A Stafford Road, Wolverhampton, engine, and a very rare visitor on the Bristol road.'

*At Bath, 28 February 1958, 6006 is in final form fitted with standard double chimney, four-row superheated boiler, mechanical lubricator forward of modified outside steam pipes, cab roof ventilator and strengthened bogie frames. Still retains original tapered-barrel buffers.*

'On the one occasion I rode on this engine in double chimney condition, I drove her up from Bath, not too well at first. But I avoided a slip in Box Tunnel, a rare non-occurrence unless sand was used. Sadly, 6006 was the first *King* to be condemned.'

# 6007
# King William III

*Built: March 1928*
*Withdrawn: September 1962*
*Mileage: 1,437,609*
*Disposal: Cox & Danks Ltd*

*Standing at Bath, 4 October 1952, with an up express. 6007 had recently been repainted green after the BR blue period. Except for a sleeved chimney the locomotive is in original condition. This engine was badly damaged in a collision at Shrivenham in 1936, and was said to have been virtually rebuilt.*

'I had only one trip on her in double chimney condition. I fired and she steamed perfectly. My note says: "A nice engine and rode beautifully".'

*At Chippenham in September 1958, fresh out of Swindon works on the evening running-in turn. The engine has received all BR modifications including a built-up double chimney, four-row superheated boiler and self-cleaning smokebox, but still retains original tapered-barrel buffers.*

# 6008
# King James II

*Built: March 1928*
*Withdrawn: June 1962*
*Mileage: 1,695,925*
*Disposal: Swindon*

*Standing in the middle road at Bath, 10 January 1953, while Driver Sid Forge oils the 'bars and glands' before returning with 6008 to Swindon.*

'I rode behind 6008 on the 4.15 pm ex-Paddington on 8 September 1953. My note says: "Early everywhere".'

*Kenneth Leech was again at Bath, 31 December 1958, to photograph 6008 on another Swindon running-in turn. The locomotive was now fully modified and fitted with a standard double chimney.*

# 6009
# King Charles II

Built: *March 1928*
Withdrawn: *September 1962*
Mileage: *1,935,102*
Disposal: *J. Cashmore Ltd*

*At Chippenham, 7 June
1951. 6009 is in original
condition, except for BR
livery and stepped inside
cylinder casing.*

*A surprisingly grimy 6009
on the Swindon running-in
turn at Chippenham, 21
October 1959. Has received
all the BR modifications,
including a standard
double chimney.*

'I rode on her with Driver J.P. Gale (Old Oak Common) on 27
October 1959. A good ride, though a bit bouncy at the back end. I
drove, 15 per cent cut off and just a crack of main port. 63mph into
Box Tunnel, 45mph out, and first port at Thingley. Altogether I had
five trips on 6009, three driving and two firing.'

*6010* King Charles I
*entering Box Tunnel,*
*13 July 1959.*

# 6010
# King Charles I

*Built: April 1928*
*Withdrawn: June 1962*
*Mileage: 1,928,258*
*Disposal: Swindon*

*A credit to Swindon. 6010 is in immaculate condition on the evening running-in turn at Chippenham, 11 October 1951, having received sleeved chimney, four-row superheated boiler, mechanical lubricator at rear of modified outside steam pipes and stepped inside cylinder cover.*

'On one occasion, when firing to 6010, I did not do well. The fire was caked and needed the use of a pricker or poker through it (beyond my scope at 66 years of age!). In 1960 I had three trips on her, and by then she was rough.'

*In final BR condition right through to parallel-barrel buffers. Chippenham, 4 April 1959.*

# 6011
# King James I

Built: April 1928
Withdrawn: December 1962
Mileage: 1,718,295
Disposal: Swindon

*Chippenham, December 1954. Sleeved chimney with four-row superheater, mechanical lubricator to rear of modified outside steam pipes, inside cylinder cover.*

*Bath, June 1957. Built-up double chimney, self cleaning smokebox, mechanical lubricator forward of modified outside steam pipes, stepped inside cylinder cover, strengthened bogie frame, cab roof ventilator.*

'No one can take photographs on the Bath "middle road" nowadays. The platform has been extended and the rail layout changed; but in 1957 one could get anything from a head-on view to a rear quarter aspect.'

## 6012
## King Edward VI

*Built: April 1928*
*Withdrawn: September 1962*
*Mileage: 1,910,525*
*Disposal: Cox & Danks Ltd*

*Running into Chippenham, 26 October 1951. In original condition except stepped inside cylinder cover and blue livery. GWR Shed Code LA (Laira) painted on framing.*

'Altogether I had ten trips on 6012, some with single chimney, some with double chimney, and only once found her other than a good engine.'

*At Bath, 15 February 1958. Standard double chimney. Four-row superheated boiler. Mechanical lubricator forward of modified outside steam pipes. Stepped inside cylinder cover. Deep covers to inside valve spindles. Strengthened bogie frames. Cab roof ventilator. Original buffers still retained.*

'The photograph recalls her as she was on a glorious "double home" trip from Paddington to Plymouth and back. On other occasions I fired on her twice and drove her four times in all.'

*6013* King Henry VIII *with the 'Bristolian', accelerating hard from a 5 mph permanent way slack due to serious landslip. Langley (Wilts) 17 December 1954.*

## 6013
## King Henry VIII

*Built: May 1928*
*Withdrawn: June 1962*
*Mileage: 1,950,462*
*Disposal: Swindon*

*A wet day at Chippenham, 21 June 1950, but 6013 still looks great, fresh out of Swindon works. Almost original condition except for stepped inside cylinder cover and blue livery. GWR shed code PDN (Paddington) on side framing.*

'I fired on her five times, usually with success, but it was Driver Charlie Brown who showed me that I could not cope with a *King* driven really hard.'

*In June 1956, fresh from Swindon with built-up double chimney, mechanical lubricator forward of modified outside steam pipes, self-cleaning smokebox, stepped inside cylinder cover, deep covers to valve spindles, strengthened bogie frame, cab roof ventilator.*

'In all, I drove this engine on five occasions. But it was with a double chimney that I had to enter in my diary, "Much humbled, I could NOT get her to steam; she beat me completely".' (17 August 1957).

# 6014
# King Henry VII

*Built: May 1928*
*Withdrawn: September 1962*
*Mileage: 1,830,386*
*Disposal: Cox & Danks Ltd*

*At Chippenham, March 1951 in blue livery. Only other BR alteration is the stepped inside cylinder cover, where also the oil trimming box and train identification number frame bracket are clearly visible. 6014 was streamlined in 1935, but all 'bits and pieces', except wedge-cab, were removed gradually.*

'Another Stafford Road engine, and a very rare visitor to Chippenham.'

*Swindon Works, September 1959. Standard double chimney, modified outside steam pipes, stepped inside cylinder cover strengthened bogie frame and parallel buffers. Still retains wedge fronted cab from 'streamlined' days. Appears to be linked temporarily to a 'Hawksworth' tender for movement within the Works.*

'The water pipes on *Kings* were larger in diameter than on all other classes, so that 6014 could not be coupled (as regards water hoses) to a Hawksworth tender. The *Kings*' tenders were special to the class.'

# 6015
# King Richard III

*Built: June 1928*
*Withdrawn: September 1962*
*Mileage: 1,901,585*
*Disposal: Cox & Danks Ltd*

*Chippenham 16 June 1951.*
*In almost original condition*
*except for stepped inside*
*cylinder cover and blue*
*livery. The smokebox door*
*step is still retained.*

'I did not ride on her in single chimney days, but have a note of runs behind her up from Chippenham to Paddington: twelve coaches; a good run, and on the same day (26 November 1952) a dull run down, load also twelve coaches, showing how often the engine crew determine the standard of performance.'

*Chippenham, December*
*1956. 6015 was the first*
*King to be fitted with a*
*double blast pipe and a*
*double chimney. The*
*chimney was the first built-*
*up steel sheet type, before*
*a cast iron pattern was*
*designed. In this form,*
*6015 was to set an*
*authentically recorded top*
*speed for a King — almost*
*109mph down Lavington*
*Bank.*

'A lovely engine, though she ran hot twice in the fourteen years of my diaries. On my first firing trip I thought I did well, considering slack coal and dirty fire. Next time I fired, and couldn't keep her quiet — flap down on floor and dampers shut. Lovely!'

# 6016
# King Edward V

*Built: June 1928*
*Withdrawn: September 1962*
*Mileage: 1,811,207*
*Disposal: J. Cashmore Ltd*

*Standing at Chippenham 14 October 1950. Blue livery and stepped inside cylinder cover are the only BR alterations. No insignia appears on tender.*

'My diary says she failed on down "Bristolian" on 9 February 1955, but she worked the up "Bristolian" all right on 28 March!'

*At Bath, 23 May 1959 with Driver 'Con' Mason, of Swindon. 6016 has all the BR modifications.*

'I fired on 6016 on 16 January 1958, when she was new out of works. She was all right for steam, but I got the idea that she would soon be run-down as the left-hand back axlebox was knocking.'

# 6017
# King Edward IV

*Built: June 1928*
*Withdrawn: July 1962*
*Mileage: 1,853,262*
*Disposal: Cox & Danks Ltd*

*Chippenham 1 April 1954, after light repairs. Sleeved chimney with self-cleaning smokebox, modified outside steam pipes, stepped inside cylinder cover and cab roof ventilators.*

*16 June 1967 in Swindon works yard. Has all the BR modifications, except that the old tapered-barrel type buffers were retained.*

'This was another occasion when an engine was posed for me by the late Stanley Morris. I only rode on 6017 once, and never had such an engine for steam. She rode beautifully, no knocks or rattles. In fact, the fireman rode in the train, so the driver must have had confidence in my ability to fire.'

*Approaching Whiteball Tunnel.*

# 6018
# King Henry VI

*Built: June 1928*
*Withdrawn: December 1962*
*Mileage: 1,738,387*
*Disposal: Swindon*

*Seen at Chippenham, 26 April 1955, with sleeved chimney, mechanical lubricator to the rear of modified outside steam pipes, and cab roof ventilators.*

'My first footplate trip on 6018 was on this day, and I drove for a short distance only, not having yet gained the confidence of enginemen. It is fair to say that in this instance the engineman drove 6018 rather harder than was my later practice on this turn.'

*Except for the original tapered-barrel buffers, 6018 has all BR modifications as she stands at Chippenham in March 1958. She was distinguished as the last* King *in BR service; and was reinstated for the final* King *run, a Stephenson Locomotive Society Special from Birmingham to Swindon works, 28 April 1963.*

'Out of six footplate trips on 6018 when fitted with double chimney, I choose the very last, on 8 September 1962. Load was thirteen coaches. I drove from Bath, and made the stop at Chippenham, nicely — there was no margin of platform length to make it safe to stop short or over-run at all. Maximum speed at Thingley was 70mph. Fire was in poor shape at Bath, so I took things easy to Box, where fire was good enough to open out on. I thought brakes were dragging a bit, so used big ejector from time to time. She was in very good condition and rode very nicely. This was the last day of the Summer Service and the last day of main line steam.'

## 6019
## King Henry V

*Built: July 1928*
*Withdrawn: September 1962*
*Mileage: 1,912,309*
*Disposal: J. Cashmore Ltd*

*Swindon Works, 16*
*November 1952. Original*
*condition except for*
*stepped inside cylinder*
*cover.*

'Another instance of the engine being posed for me by Stanley Morris. I did not ride on this engine in single chimney days.'

*Swindon Shed, 14*
*December 1958. All BR*
*modifications except*
*original buffers. Swindon*
*Shed Foreman Arthur*
*Horley on footplate*

'Seven bogie coaches was a featherweight load for a *King,* and as an example of how lightly they could be worked and yet keep ahead of time, I quote an instance of my driving 6019 from Bath to Chippenham all the way, including the two miles up at 1 in 100 through Box Tunnel, on the first port, or pilot valve, of the regulator. The main valve was not opened at all, yet the speed was 60mph at Box on 16 per cent cut off. The cut off was increased to 20 per cent through the tunnel, and brought back to 15 per cent thereafter. The speed at Thingley was 65mph.'

## 6020
## King Henry IV

*Built: May 1930*
*Withdrawn: July 1962*
*Mileage: 1,686,568*
*Disposal: Cox & Danks Ltd*

*17 March 1954, Chippenham. Four-row superheater and mechanical lubricator to rear of original outside steam pipes. Still retains original chimney.*

*At Chippenham 21 June 1961, 6020 has all BR modifications.*

'Photographed after my only footplate trip on her. I fired, and built-up a big fire, but it was a blazing hot day and I sweated. The driver "put her up to 70mph after Thingley". This was my twenty-ninth *King*, 6014 being the thirtieth and last.'

# 6021
# King Richard II

*Built: June 1930*
*Withdrawn: September 1962*
*Mileage: 1,793,439*
*Disposal: J. Cashmore Ltd*

*In BR blue livery, standing in Chippenham 28 May 1951. Original condition except for stepped inside cylinder cover. GWR Shed code PDN (Paddington) painted on frame.*

'I had a good run behind her on the 6.30pm ex-Paddington on 16 April 1955, when the load was 434 tons (fourteen coaches) and we arrived at Chippenham on time in spite of seven minutes signal delays. My diary reads that O.S. Nock, who was travelling with me, took all particulars!'

*Chippenham, March 1957. In final BR condition except for original buffers.*

'I had three trips on this engine in double chimney condition, two driving and one firing. Of one of the driving trips I noted that she was a strong engine: of the other I commented that "though a nice engine, knock in the back axle boxes was just noticeable." Firing to her, "she was a lovely engine, steamed with flap on floor, though coal poor. Rode beautifully, no knocks or rattles. Slipped in Box Tunnel at usual place."'

# 6022
# King Edward III

*Built: June 1930*
*Withdrawn: September 1962*
*Mileage: 1,733,189*
*Disposal: Cox & Danks Ltd*

*Chippenham 26 March 1953. Still retains original chimney and outside steam pipes. Mechanical lubricator in rear position, stepped inside cylinder cover. Blue livery. Train identification numbers in frame attached to smokebox door handles. First King to receive four-row superheater in 1948.*

'I was officially invited to Swindon when she got her four-row superheater. It was on this occasion that I first met Stanley Morris, and this led to a strong friendship and many photographs subsequently.'

*Chippenham 5 June 1956. First pattern built-up double chimney, self-cleaning smokebox, mechanical lubricator forward of modified outside steam pipes, stepped inside cylinder cover, cab roof ventilator and strengthened bogie frame.*

'The trickle of steam apparently from the front end of outside cylinder is actually from the drainpipe of the vacuum ejector exhaust. On a driving trip on her I noted: "Very nice engine, rode well and no rattles, but gave me the impression that she would be really 'gay' in a few months' time." '

## 6023
## King Edward II

*Built: June 1930*
*Withdrawn: June 1962*
*Mileage: 1,554,201*
*Disposal: Woodham Bros, Barry, South Wales. Still not cut up in 1979.*

*On the Swindon running-in turn at Bath, 5 December 1951, in BR blue livery. Original chimney and outside steam pipes retained although having received four-row superheater and mechanical lubricator (in rear position). Stepped inside cylinder cover.*

*Chippenham, June 1957. In final condition except for original buffers.*

'On the five trips I had on this engine in double chimney condition I drove twice and fired once. On the latter occasion, on 15 August 1957, I noted that she was a lovely engine and steamed well with the flap on the floor; and on a trip in 1958, when I "watched the fireman", my comment was similar.'

## 6024
## King Edward I

*Built: June 1930*
*Withdrawn: June 1962*
*Mileage: 1,570,015*
*Disposal: Woodham Bros,*
*Barry, South Wales.*
*Purchased by the King*
*Preservation Society. Moved*
*to Quainton Road in 1973 for*
*eventual restoration.*

*Middle road at Bath, 18*
*November 1950. Still in*
*original condition except*
*for stepped inside cylinder*
*cover and in blue livery.*

'The circumferential streaks on the boiler indicate she had "lifted" the safety valves and "blown-off" with foamy, probably oily, water in the boiler, perhaps in the running shed, but almost certainly while standing and not while moving.'

*Chippenham 27 March*
*1957. In final condition*
*with all BR modifications,*
*but retaining original*
*buffers.*

'On 1 September 1959, I rode up on 6024 from Bath to Chippenham. I drove, but slipped twice in starting from Bath. The regulator was very stiff and awkward. Load was nine bogies, so first port of regulator was just not good enough. 15 per cent cut off, except 18 per cent in Box Tunnel, with regulator well back. A strong engine and not too rough.'

## 6025
## King Henry III

*Built: July 1930*
*Withdrawn: December 1962*
*Mileage: 1,836,713*
*Disposal: Swindon*

*Standing in Bath, July 1955. Sleeved chimney, mechanical lubricator rear of outside steam pipes, stepped inside cylinder cover and cab roof ventilator.*

'A Laira (Plymouth) engine that had the reputation of being strongest of all the *King*s, but to me, with limited experience, I thought 6019 was better.'

*Bath 23 March 1957, in final condition with all BR modifications except for original buffers, and mechanical lubricator still in rear position.*

'Perhaps my view of 6025 was coloured by a brief attempt on one occasion at firing to her: "I fired to Bathford and then gave up. Fireman had to put pricker through, and I drove. A strong engine, but signals spoiled the trip." '

# 6026
# King John

*Built: July 1930*
*Withdrawn: September 1962*
*Mileage: 1,622,350*
*Disposal: Swindon*

*Except for stepped inside cylinder casing, still in original condition. Blue livery with no insignia on tender. Bath 18 June 1952.*

'On learning that 6026 was Mr R.A. Smeddle's favourite *King,* but that he had no photograph of her, I sent him a print of this view. However, I heard later that the next time she was repainted, he had had an official photograph taken of her.'

*Chippenham 8 March 1958 with all BR modifications, but retains original buffers.*

'This was the engine I failed to get to steam. On one occasion I noted "I fired and did badly, fire may have been dirty. 200lb and half a glass, might have been worse." And on another trip, later; "Again I could not make her steam, but coal was slack and bad."'

## 6027
## King Richard I

*Built: July 1930*
*Withdrawn: September 1962*
*Mileage: 1,836,535*
*Disposal: Cox & Danks Ltd*

*Sleeved chimney, mechanical lubricator to rear of modified outside steam pipes, stepped inside cylinder cover, cab roof ventilator. Bath 18 January 1955.*

'In this condition, I rode up from Bath on her, just firing one round to Bathford, and driving thence. I drove at 18 per cent cut off through Box Tunnel with the regulator well back, and then 15 per cent. Rode very nicely, but a little livelier and much softer than an LNER A4 on which I had ridden two days previously.'

*At Chippenham 6 September 1956. First type of double chimney mechanical lubricator forward of modified outside steam pipes, stepped inside cylinder cover, strengthened bogie frame and cab roof ventilator.*

'I had a grand ride up from Plymouth to Chippenham with Driver Charlie Brown on this engine. I fired from Newton Abbot to Exeter, but as Fireman Holder reminded me, that was over the only easy bit of the road! Still, she steamed all right.'

## 6028
## King George VI

*Built: July 1930*
*Withdrawn: November 1962*
*Mileage: 1,663,271*
*Disposal: Birds (Swansea)*
*Ltd, Risca*

*Bath 15 March 1952. In light blue livery, but retaining original chimney and outside steam pipes, although fitted with four-row superheater. Mechanical lubricator in rear position, stepped inside cylinder cover. Also carries bogie with the slotted frontplate frame. Named* King Henry II *until 1937.*

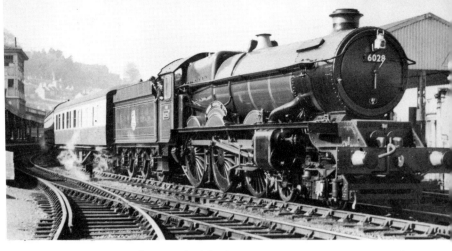

'I have two notes of runs behind 6028 on the 8.26am up from Chippenham. In 1951 she gained about seven minutes, in 1953 we arrived twenty-five minutes late, which looks like trouble on the engine since there was no mention of traffic delays or fog in my diary.'

'I drove her three times, once on a stopping train in the pitch dark. The platforms were not lit, so that judgment in stopping just right was not easy. On another occasion, I set the reverser in 15 per cent cut off most of the way, but she was riding pretty gaily at over 60mph, and we only had half a glass of water most of the way.'

# 6029
# King Edward VIII

*Built: August 1930*
*Withdrawn: July 1962*
*Mileage: 1,859,278*
*Disposal: J. Cashmore Ltd*

*Chippenham, 1 November 1951. In original condition except for stepped inside cylinder cover. Named* King Stephen *until 1936.*

'As an example of how short a period can elapse after an engine has the light repairs called "soling and heeling", 6029 was out, soled and heeled, on 9 March 1953, and then out again, this time after a heavy repair and repainted, on 7 October 1953.'

*Leaving Chippenham in January 1957, in almost final condition. Had yet to receive standard pattern double chimney.*

'Only once was I on the footplate of this engine and on that occasion my diary read: "Back from Bath with Cyril Palmer; I drove; no comments!" The sad early death of Cyril Palmer reminds me that in all cases where I have mentioned the name of a driver I was riding with, that driver is now no longer living — except in memory. Altogether, I had 113 trips, long and short, on *King*s, on fifty-eight of which I drove, and on forty-one of which I fired. How lucky I was.'

# Kingdom of the Footplate

The photographs on the following pages have been selected from Kenneth Leech's vast collection of footplate portraits. To him they are of far greater interest than any of his locomotive photographs, for it was his friendship with the men of the footplate that resulted in so many years of his retirement being spent driving and firing steam engines almost every day.

This collection of photographs constitutes an incomparable and unrepeatable social document now that the steam engine driver and his fireman mate have vanished from the everyday railway scene. They were a rare breed, used to working in twosomes in a confined and alien environment, conversation curtailed by percussive vibration and noise all the time the engine was moving. The job demanded great powers of concentration either mentally on signals and the road ahead, or physically on the task of shifting tons of coal from tender into firebox. In summer enginemen sweated; in winter they were roasted in front and frozen behind. Theirs was a man's job in the fullest sense.

Once upon the footplate the driver was in charge of the locomotive. He worked by the Rule Book; he understood his engine in all its moods and knew the regular road like the back of his hand. He was always aware of his responsibilities, for the safety of his train and its passengers. Drivers were not only characters — they were men of great character.

Drivers and firemen came in all shapes and sizes; all were different in physical appearance and individual manner of dress. Even so, it is possible to describe a typical engine driver as being a man in his middle fifties, of medium height, usually wearing a regulation cap, a collar and tie, overall trousers and buttoned jacket. Being older than his fireman he looked to be the man in charge, but his years of toiling on the shovel and his heavier responsibilities showed in his work-worn face.

By contrast, firemen were usually slimmer, more wiry in build, and often they sported a diversity of working attire. Head-gear varied from regulation cap, service beret, Commando-style knitted hat, green jungle cap to simple knotted handkerchief. But the archetypal locomotive fireman could be summed up as one wearing a slop jacket tucked into his trousers, braces outside. His coat pinned at the neck, cycle clips around his trouser bottoms, and a pad of cotton waste in his hand. In later years on BR he often wore goggles as protection against the fine dust from ovoids and inferior coal.

Certainly, but for his wonderful rapport with enginemen and inspectors all over the Western Region, Kenneth Leech's unofficial footplate journeyings would never have taken place, and it is possible that many of his superb locomotive photographs might not have been taken.

*6018 King Henry VI at Paddington. Special test run of the 'Bristolian'.*

Driver Bill Bateman and Fireman Ron Thompson. Kenneth Leech rode with Bill Bateman more than with any other enginemen. They did 130 trips together, and still keep in touch.

Driver Charlie Brown smiles knowingly, having just beaten Kenneth Leech with 6013. Inspector Jenkins tries to look serious while Kenneth takes the photograph.

Pipe smoking Driver Tommy Worth, who retired rather than drive diesels, seems very relaxed, but Fireman Sarney (a very good fireman indeed) could be a fugitive actor from a Pinewood wartime film epic!

Driver Vincent sits down for his photograph to be taken, but his Fireman already has his gloves on, and seems impatient to set-to with his shovel.

Driver Joe Ward and his Fireman looking
very neat and tidy on the footplate of 6000
*King George V.*

Cheerful two-some. Driver Williams is sedately attired, but his mate adopts a buccaneering attitude with his knotted handkerchief.

It's a long way down to the ground! Driver Percy Steer favours an old-style golfing cap, but still keeps his jacket buttoned-up.

Swindon's Herbert Lee characterizes the archetypal Great Western fireman: jacket tucked into trousers, braces outside, and collar pinned. He wears clips around his trouser bottoms — and has a waste pad in his hand. Driver Frank Yeates looks ready for the 'off'.

A typical Western Region footplate scene. The fireman wears goggles because of the fire dust from eggs or ovoids. His shovel handle is held high, the blade straight. Note the clean firebox front, and the Cockney tea can and cups. (Photograph taken on 6012)

On the footplate of 6027, Driver Charlie Brown looks highly amused at the prospect of having 'Fireman' Leech with him from North Road, Plymouth to Chippenham, although Kenneth Leech's firing was done only between Taunton and Exeter on this trip, since he had already ridden on the footplate from Paddington to Plymouth, and Fireman Holder, Charlie's mate was fresh.
In his younger days, Charlie Brown had been the fireman on record-breaking trips with the 'Cheltenham Flyer'. He must have packed a punch on the shovel.

'Now what's all this about?' the fireman seems to be asking Kenneth Leech. But Driver Colin (Con) Mason has seen it all before.

Driver Smitherman and 'Fireman' Kenneth Leech (right) with 6012 at Taunton, 25 July 1961. Chief Inspector Andress took the photograph.

Driver Walter Harris was held in great
esteem by all his mates, they thought him
one of the finest drivers on the 'Western'.
Certainly Walter Harris was a first-class
engineman and Kenneth Leech observed:
'He was always altering the setting of the
cut-off to suit the road. He must have
saved the company a great deal of coal!'

*Down 'Cornish Riviera'*
*diverted via Chippenham.*
*9 May 1954.*

*'Royal Duchy' at Savernake.*

# The 'Kings' were withdrawn in 1962

'. . . no more would they blast out of Box Tunnel, whistle screaming, smoke and steam clouds billowing above the tree tops, sunlight glinting on their copper crowns.'